Leipzig
Travel Guide

Quick Trips Series

No part of this publication may be reproduced, stored in a retrieval system, or transmitted, in any form or by any means without the prior written permission of the publisher, nor be otherwise circulated in any form of binding or cover other than that in which it is published and without similar condition being imposed on the subsequent purchaser. If there are any errors or omissions in copyright acknowledgements the publisher will be pleased to insert the appropriate acknowledgement in any subsequent printing of this publication. Although we have taken all reasonable care in researching this book we make no warranty about the accuracy or completeness of its content and disclaim all liability arising from its use.

Copyright © 2016, Astute Press
All Rights Reserved.

Table of Contents

LEIPZIG — 5
- 🌐 CUSTOMS & CULTURE 7
- 🌐 GEOGRAPHY 10
- 🌐 WEATHER & BEST TIME TO VISIT 13

SIGHTS & ACTIVITIES: WHAT TO SEE & DO — 14
- 🌐 THOMASKIRCHE (ST. THOMAS CHURCH) 15
- 🌐 BACH ARCHIVE & MUSEUM 19
- 🌐 OLD TOWN HALL & MUSEUM 23
- 🌐 COURTYARDS & PASSAGEWAYS 25
- 🌐 MONUMENT TO THE BATTLE OF THE NATIONS 26
- 🌐 LEIPZIG MUSIC TRAIL 27
- 🌐 LEIPZIG ZOO 29
- 🌐 MUSEUM IN THE ROUND CORNER 31

BUDGET TIPS — 35
- 🌐 ACCOMMODATION 35
  - Gastehaus Leipzig 35
  - Mercure Leipzig am Johannisplatz 36
  - Hotel Adler 37
  - Hotel Admiral Leipzig 38
  - Hotel Royal International 38
- 🌐 PLACES TO EAT 39

    Zill's Tunnel 39
    Tobagi 40
    Coffe Baum 41
    Zest 42
    Villers 43

🌐 Shopping 44

    Christmas Market 44
    Flea Market 44
    Central Station Promenade 45
    Hofe am Bruhl 45
    Nova Eventis 46

KNOW BEFORE YOU GO   47

🌐 **Entry Requirements** 47

🌐 **Health Insurance** 47

🌐 **Travelling with Pets** 48

🌐 **Airports** 49

  🌐 **Airlines** 51

🌐 **Currency** 52

🌐 **Banking & ATMs** 52

🌐 **Credit Cards** 53

🌐 **Reclaiming VAT** 53

🌐 **Tipping Policy** 54

🌐 **Mobile Phones** 55

🌐 **Dialling Code** 55

🌐 **Emergency Numbers** 56

🌐 **Public Holidays** 56

🌐 **Time Zone** 57

🌐 **Daylight Savings Time** 57

- School Holidays 57
- Trading Hours 58
- Driving Laws 58
- Smoking Laws 59
- Drinking Laws 60
- Electricity 60
- Tourist Information (TI) 61
- Food & Drink 61
- Websites 63

LEIPZIG TRAVEL GUIDE

Leipzig

Located in the Federal State of Saxony, the city of Leipzig is a popular tourist destination in eastern Germany. Not only is it ranked as one of the most livable cities in the country, Leipzig was also ranked as a city with one of the 'highest quality of living in Europe'. The city's fortune declined during the Communist era, but 'the Boomtown of eastern Germany' made a stunning turnaround after the

LEIPZIG TRAVEL GUIDE

end of the Cold War, to emerge as one of the most significant cultural, economic, and tourism centers of Germany. The New York Times listed it as a must visit city a few years ago in 2010.

The earliest record of Leipzig dates back to 1015 making it at least 1000 years old. It was originally known by the Slavic name – Lipsk. The city is situated at the confluence of 3 rivers – Pleisse, Parthe, and White Elster.

Leipzig became a significant commercial hub in Europe for its location at the intersection of Via Imperii and Via Regia – 2 of the most important medieval trade routes. Another claim to fame for Leipzig is the early 19th century Battle of Leipzig, the largest battle in Europe before the World Wars. The historic battle ended the presence of Napoleon in Germany. From being one of the largest

LEIPZIG TRAVEL GUIDE

publishing centers in medieval Europe to being home to one of the oldest universities of the country, the city of Leipzig has also been a major center for culture in Germany. Its 18th century classical literary movement earned it the nickname – Klein Paris or Little Paris.

With major improvements in its tourism infrastructure, the multi-faceted city of Leipzig today offers a vast array of attractions to its visitors. Tourists are treated to many historic monuments and refurbished medieval architecture. Festivals, theaters, and literary events crowd the culture calendar of the city throughout the year. Families can visit the numerous museums, the famous Leipzig Zoo, and many of the nature parks in and around the city. The unique passageways and shopping centers make it a haven for shopaholics. As it is a university town, there is no dearth of nighttime entertainment. From live music and traditional pubs to trendy restaurants and new age dance clubs, sun-down Leipzig is a lively treat of its own. With so many attractions and activities all round the year, Leipzig never disappoints.

🌐 Customs & Culture

Birthplace of Richard Wagner, workplace of Bach, and university town of Goethe – the city of Leipzig has had a long tryst with the best of the cultural scene of the nation.

The cultural fame of Leipzig is not limited to its history. The multi-award winning St Thomas Choir, founded in 1212, still performs regularly to packed houses! Amongst its many famous conductors was the legendary Johann Sebastian Bach. The MDR Leipzig Radio Symphony Orchestra, founded in 1923, is not only the oldest radio orchestra in Germany, but one of the oldest in the world. It

LEIPZIG TRAVEL GUIDE

has many memorable performances over the decades including playing twice for the Pope – in 1993 and in 2003. Another famous orchestra is the Leipzig Gewandhaus Orchestra, named after the Gewandhaus Concert Hall where it is based. This orchestra, founded in 1781, performs regularly at the Thomaskirche and the Leipzig Opera. The annual Bach Festival is a major classical music festival that celebrates the music of the composer who lived and worked here from 1723 to 1750.

For those looking for more contemporary music can attend the annual summertime Wave-Gotik-Treffen, the largest Gothic Festival in the world. Apart from the performance of over 150 musical bands, the festival also has a Gothic village and stalls selling Gothic merchandise. The heavy metal and independent music scene is also very popular in Leipzig. Other popular

LEIPZIG TRAVEL GUIDE

annual events include the electronic music festival – Ladyfest Leipzeg, jazz festival – Jazztage, and the pop music festival – Leipzig Pop Up.

Art lovers can visit not only visit the art museums in the city, they can also attend exhibitions and workshops at any of the numerous galleries spread across the city. One of the most popular venues is the Plagwitz – an old refurbished factory building that houses nearly a dozen galleries. The Gallery of Contemporary Art exhibits and promotes German art in the whole of Europe. Other popular galleries include the Sparkasse, Halle 14, and the VNG.

The cultural-event calendar of Leipzig has a number of annual events that attract a large footfall from people of all ages. The Leipzig Book Fair is second only to the

LEIPZIG TRAVEL GUIDE

Frankfurt Book Fair in terms of size and stalls. The city has many trade shows, the most popular and oldest being the Leipzig Fair, dating back over 800 years! Leipzig also has a very strong revue and cabaret scene with many patrons crowning it the cabaret capital of Germany. The Humor and Satire Festival and the Laughter Fair are 2 major events with many top-quality cabaret shows, and a variety of comedy, music, and aerial acrobatics performances.

🌎 Geography

Leipzig is located in central eastern Germany about 150 km south of the capital Berlin. It is about 100 km from Dresden, the largest city in the Federal State of Saxony. Other popular cities close to Leipzig include Halle (32 km), Magdeburg (101 km), Brunswick (163 km), and Prague (200 km).

LEIPZIG TRAVEL GUIDE

Leipzig is served by the Leipzig/Halle Airport - https://www.leipzig-halle-airport.de/en/, IATA: LEJ. It is one of the largest airports in the country and second only to the airports in Berlin in eastern Germany. The airport is served by many major and low cost airlines that connect Leipzig to many cities across the globe including Vienna, Paris, Amsterdam, Istanbul, Antalya, and Rhodes, to name a few. It is located about 22 km from the city center and is connected by shuttle, train, taxi, and rental car service. Trains are the quickest (less than 15 minutes) and reasonably cheap costing about €5 for the ride to the city center.

A ride to Leipzig in a train will bring one to the Leipzig Hauptbahnhof – the largest railway terminal in Europe. It has 28 platforms including to 2 underground tunnel

LEIPZIG TRAVEL GUIDE

platforms. Equipped with a large shopping mall and numerous connections across Europe, the station is abuzz with activity throughout the day. The German Railway - http://www.bahn.de/p/view/index.shtml runs a number of connections to Leipzig from various cities including Berlin (80 min, €43), Frankfurt (3.5 hrs, €72), Dresden (90 min, €20), and Prague (4.5 hrs, €50).

Driving in to Leipzig is an option because of the excellent road conditions. The city is connected to the A9, A14, and A38 motorways. The city has an extensive Car-Park Routing System to help visiting drivers, details of which can be found at the Tourist Information Center – on Richard Wagner Strasse near the train station.

Those preferring to take the bus can use a number of services including Berlinlinienbus -

LEIPZIG TRAVEL GUIDE

https://www.berlinlinienbus.de/, Meinfernbus - http://meinfernbus.de/, and Eurolines - http://www.eurolines.com/en/. These bus services connect Leipzig to practically almost all corners of Europe.

Once in the city, visitors can use the widely used public transport – buses and trams - to move around. These are run by the LVB and MDV. A single trip ticket is priced at €2.40. It is recommended to buy a day ticket or family ticket as it usually turns out to be much cheaper. Night transport is also available on certain routes. For those planning to use the taxi or drive should keep in mind that the city center is a no-auto zone, and is best covered by foot. Cycling is common in and around Leipzig. The city has a number of bike rentals, one of the most popular being http://www.nextbike.de/en/. There are also many bike tours - http://www.radfahren-in-leipzig.de/ in Leipzig.

🌐 Weather & Best Time to Visit

Leipzig has an Oceanic Climate with mild summers and cold to very cold winters. Temperatures in the summer months (May to Sep) reach an average high of around 22 degrees Celsius and an average low of around 12 degrees. The winter months (Nov to Feb) are much cooler.

Average temperatures rise to around 3 to 4 degrees Celsius and fall well below freezing – around -2 to -3 degrees. Rain is constant throughout the year with slightly heavier showers in the summer months. July and August are the wettest months with about 65 mm of rain. Although Leipzig is a popular attraction all the year round,

LEIPZIG TRAVEL GUIDE

the warmer temperatures in the summer months, especially May to August, make it the best time to visit the city.

LEIPZIG TRAVEL GUIDE

Sights & Activities: What to See & Do

Tourists visiting Leipzig can opt for the Leipzig Card. The card can be bought for 1 adult (1-day or 3-day) or for a family (2 adults and up to 3 children below 14 years of age). The 1-day card (€9.90), 3-day card (€19.90), and the family 3-day card (€37.90) is for free public transport, and discounts at a number of museums, family parks and attractions, restaurants, and shopping centers. The

Leipzig Card can be bought from the Tourist Information Center or online at

http://www.leipzig.travel/en/Plan_your_stay/LEIPZIG_CARD_2054.html.

🌐 Thomaskirche (St. Thomas Church)

The Thomaskirche is a Lutheran Church located in the city center of Leipzig. It is one of the most popular tourist attractions in the city. Not only is it a place of worship, the church is also witness to many historic events in the city. It is home to the St Thomas Choir – Thomanerchor. Founded in 1212, it is one of the oldest choirs in the world. The choir was directed by the legendary Bach from 1923 until his death in 1950. The church is also the final resting place of the composer. There is a statue of Bach next to the church to honor the maestro.

LEIPZIG TRAVEL GUIDE

The origin of the present church dates back to the 12th century when it was a part of the St Thomas Monastery. Excavations around the altar of the church revealed that there was originally a Romanesque styled church in the area. At that time it was affiliated to the Augustinian order. The present building came up sometime around the late 15th century in a Gothic style of architecture. One of the highlights in the history of the church was the preaching by renowned reformer Martin Luther on the Pentecost Sunday of 1539. The church went through some major repairs in the late 19th century which added some neo-Gothic features to the building. The church received a second major and much needed repair after the unification of GDR and FDR in the 1990s. The restoration was completed in 2000 and coincided with the 250 death anniversary of Bach.

LEIPZIG TRAVEL GUIDE

The church presently reaches a height of 76 m with a tower that is 68 m tall.

The nave is 50 m in length, 25 m in width, and 18 m in height. At an angle of 63 degrees, the roof of the church is one of the steepest in Germany. The church is nearly 7 storeys high and dominates the skyline in the city center.

The interior of the church is decorated with statues and paintings from the Bible. There are 2 organs – the late 19th century Sauer Organ and the new Bach Organ built in 2000. The Bach Organ is a replica of the organ that Bach used to play when he was associated with the church. The glass windows are an artistic feature of the church. The original windows were of plain glass and were replaced with colored glass during the restoration in

LEIPZIG TRAVEL GUIDE

the late 19th century. These colored-glass windows were damaged during the World War II and had to be reinstalled in 2000. Visitors can see the new installations on the south side of the church which are dedicated to Kaiser Wilhelm I, Johann Bach, Martin Luther, Adolf of Sweden, King Gustav II, and the fallen soldiers of World War I. The bell tower of the church has 4 bells; the oldest and heaviest called the Gloriosa. With a diameter of 2.04 m and weighing 5200 kg, the bell was cast in 1477.

There have been a number of historic events at the Thomaskirche. In December 1409, the Leipzig University was founded at the St Thomas Monastery making it one of the oldest universities in Germany. In May 1789, Mozart played the organ in the church.

LEIPZIG TRAVEL GUIDE

In 1806, Napoleon's troops used the church to store munitions. The building was used as a hospital during the historic Battle of Leipzig. In August 1813, renowned composer Richard Wagner was baptized in Thomaskirche; 15 years later in 1928, Wagner returned to study piano at the same place. In 1950, the remains of Bach were moved from his original resting place at Johanneskirche to the nave of the Thomaskirche as the former was severely damaged by the Allied bombing of World War II. His grave can be seen at the nave of the church.

The Thomaskirche is open from 9 am to 6 pm. Guided tours are conducted by the church staff through prior appointment at a fee of €1 per person. The church tower is open to visitors only on Saturdays and Sundays between March and November. It offers excellent panoramic views of the city. There is an entry fee of €2.

🌐 Bach Archive & Museum

Leipzig has been one of the major cultural hubs of Germany for many centuries. It has hosted many great artists, but none as famous as the legendary composer Johan Sebastian Bach who lived and worked here between 1723 and 1750. The Bach Archive – recognized by the German government as a 'cultural beacon of national importance' - was set up in Leipzig to honor and research the work of Bach. It not only researches the work of the composer but also connects with the public through the Bach Museum.

The Bach Archive is a part of the University of Leipzig. It has, under its wings, a research institute, a museum, a

LEIPZIG TRAVEL GUIDE

library, and an events department. The Archive is housed in the Bach Complex at the St Thomas Square, opposite the Thomaskirche where the composer served as a cantor for 27 years. The Archive was set up in 1950 to commemorate the 200th death anniversary of Bach. It has, over the decades, established itself as the foremost institute in the world to study, analyze, showcase, and promote the work and life of the maestro. It is a nonprofit corporation funded by the federal government, the state of Saxony, and the City of Leipzig.

The Bach Museum is spread across an exhibition area of about 450 sq m in the Bose House at the St Thomas Square. The Bose family was neighbors and friends of the Bach family. The museum has a number of sections tracing the Bach family, Bach's music, and his instruments and documents. Visitors to the museum are

LEIPZIG TRAVEL GUIDE

greeted by a marble bust of the composer that was created by Karl Ludwig Sefner in 1897. In the first section, visitors are introduced to the family tree of Bach. The family tree was made by Bach himself to highlight the contribution of his musical dynasty.

Bach's family was one of the most prominent musical dynasties that shaped German music for over 200 years! Unfortunately, although most of the 53 male members that Bach documented in his family tree were musicians, music faded out of the Bach family less than a century after his death! The centerpiece display in the room is an organ. Records state that Bach inspected and approved this organ while he was a cantor at Thomaskirche. The next section of the museum is an interactive display of Bach's Orchestra. Bach experimented with many instruments throughout his lifetime and visitors get to

LEIPZIG TRAVEL GUIDE

listen to the sounds and ensemble of those instruments. Instruments on display include a violone and a viaola d'armore that were used by musicians under his direction.

The tour of the museum then moves to the section on Bach's family home. One of the interesting displays is an iron chest bearing the monogram of Bach. The chest was used as a collection box in the Meissen Cathedral Museum as recent as 2009! An observant visitor identified the monogram and the historical significance of the chest which was then moved to its present location. The next section of the museum is – Bach and Music at Court. The section highlights Bach's relation with the royal families and the many royal titles that were conferred on him including the Dresden Court Composer. The Bach in Leipzig section displays the life and works of Bach during the 27 years he lived in Leipzig.

LEIPZIG TRAVEL GUIDE

The audio-visual sections that follow have many movies and documentaries on the composer. The Treasure Room displays documents and music sheets of Bach, many of which are so fragile that those are replaced multiple times every year. It includes 44 original choral cantatas by Bach, one of the most prized possessions of the museum. The final section of the tour has on display items that were found in the graves of Bach and Magdalena – his wife.

Other than the Bach Museum, the Bach Archive is involved with organizing the popular annual Bach Festival. It manages the library and the research institute at the same premises. The Archive also organizes a number of seminars, concerts, workshops, and publications throughout the year. There is a souvenir shop where they sell a wide variety of gift items like pencils, erasers, hand-fans, tote-bags, mugs, and magnets bearing the image or impression of Bach.

The Bach Museum is open from Tuesday to Sunday from 10 am to 4 pm. There is an entry fee of €8 with discounts for children and groups. It has free entry on the first Tuesday of every month.

🌍 Old Town Hall & Museum

Built in 1556, the Old Town Hall – Altes Rathaus - is located in the Market Square in the city center. It was built replacing a medieval building on the same spot, a reason why it is not located exactly in the center of the façade even though it is the main building of the Marktplatz.

LEIPZIG TRAVEL GUIDE

The Town Hall was constructed in less than a year under the direction of architect Hieronymus Lotter. It is built in a simple Renaissance style with a neo-Gothic tower. The original building and tower suffered extensive damage during the World War II but was restored to its former look and glory within 1950. The Town Hall houses the city museum, a restaurant, and a gift store. It is one of the most visited attractions in the city.

The Town Hall is often regarded as the 'heart of the Stadtgeschichtliches Museum'. It was founded in 1909 and showcases the history and life of the city of Leipzig. The tour of the museum starts with the historic section – 'From medieval times to the Battle of Leipzig'. With 1200 exhibits set in its historic ballrooms and chambers, it transports the visitor to the early days of the city. There is a 3-dimensional model of the city from 1823. The council chamber has many original furnishings and silverware. The vaults display the prison cells and many torture and execution instruments from the medieval days. The new section forms the 2nd half of the tour and is housed on the second floor. It focuses on the history of Leipzig from the 19th century to the present times. The section is divided into 8 categories detailing events that shaped the city in the recent decades.

The museum is open from Tuesday to Sunday from 10 am to 6 pm. The treasury and jail are open only on the 2nd and 4th Thursdays at 4pm. There is an entry of €6 with discounts for children and groups.

🌐 Courtyards & Passageways

A very unique and popular attraction of Leipzig is its courtyards and passageways. These courtyards and

LEIPZIG TRAVEL GUIDE

passageways house many exhibitions and shops highlighting Leipzig's famed history as a city of trade fairs. Most of these are concentrated in the city center. They have not only been maintained, new ones have been added over the years. Although there are commercial streets in many parts of Europe, the covered passageways and the intertwining network that one can see in Leipzig is quite unmatched. Many of these passageways were built in the medieval period, nearly 500 years ago. Today, they have been modernized, covered, and given a very chic look, but nothing has diminished the charm of these passageways. A stroll through these courtyards and passageways is not only a great way to enjoy the history of the city; it is also a delight for shopaholics considering the number of stores that are lined along these paths.

LEIPZIG TRAVEL GUIDE

A good place to start the tour of the passageways is at the Old Town Hall. Facing the front of the Town Hall is a number of passageways including the refurbished Messehofpassage, the historic Konigshauspassage, the stunningly beautiful and grand Maddler Passage, the early 20th century Theaterpassage, and the newly built Strohsackpassage. Those located to the back of the Old Town Hall include the lavish early 20th century Dussmann Passage, the artistic Ritterpassage and Bruhl Arcade, and the refurbished Handwerkerpassage.

🌐 Monument to the Battle of the Nations

Located about 6 km south east of the Leipzig city center, the Monument to the Battle of the Nations is one of the largest and tallest memorials in Europe. It was built in 1913 to commemorate the centenary of the victory in the

LEIPZIG TRAVEL GUIDE

Battle of Leipzig – also known as the Battle of the Nations. The battle, the bloodiest in Europe before the World Wars, was decisive for Germany as it marked the retreat of Napoleon the Great. A small memorial was built in 1863 to mark the 50th anniversary, exactly at the spot where the battle was fought the fiercest and where Napoleon ordered the retreat. 50 years later, on the 100th anniversary, the present monument was unveiled.

The memorial spreads over 9.9 acres. The monument has a base of 124 sq m and rises to a height of 91 m. It is made of granite and sandstone and is shaped like a pyramid with statutes adorning its exterior. The viewing tower of the memorial has beautiful panoramic views of the surrounding landscape.

LEIPZIG TRAVEL GUIDE

The memorial can be reached by Tram 15 from the central station. It is open from 10 am to 6 pm with reduced hours in the winter months. There is an entry fee of €8 with discounts for children and groups.

🌑 Leipzig Music Trail

Leipzig has a historic lineage of music. It has been the home and workplace of some of the greatest German musicians and composers.

The 5 km Leipzig Music Trail links some of the most important music-related sites in Leipzig. The trail winds in and around the city center and can be covered on foot. One can start at the New Gewandhaus at the Augustplatz. This is the base for the Gewandhaus Orchestra as well as a popular venue for many major concerts. Across the street are the MDR Studios and the

LEIPZIG TRAVEL GUIDE

Paulinum Auditorium. Behind the Augustplatz at Goldschmidtstrasse is the Mendelssohn House – former residence of the renowned German composer. Further down the street are the Edward Grieg Memorial – dedicated to the Norwegian composer, and the Peter's Music Library. Northwards near Pragerstrasse is the Grassi Museum of Musical Instruments.

The neighboring Dorrienstrasse has the Graphics Quarter – home to some of the oldest music publishers in Europe. The end of the street – walking eastwards – takes one to the Wagner Memorial and the Leipzig Opera. One can then walk along the Grimmaischestrasse that leads to the Bach Museum. To its north is the Hotel de Saxe which not only hosted many famous artists like Mozart, but was also a popular concert venue. Next to the hotel is the iconic Coffee House which has been frequented by any

LEIPZIG TRAVEL GUIDE

celebrities over the years including Richard Wagner, Robert Schumann, and Edvard Grieg. Each of these locations has audio samples that one can listen to for interesting trivia and facts on the attraction.

🌍 Leipzig Zoo

The Leipzig Zoo was opened to the public in 1878. The City of Leipzig took over its control in 1920.

Covering nearly 56 acres, the zoo has a collection of over 850 different species. It is especially famous for its carnivore exhibits like lions, Siberian tigers, and bears. It has one of the largest exhibits of great apes in the world. The zoo is also renowned for its artificially made habitats for the animals, especially the Asian elephant enclosure, the Siberian tiger enclosure, and the newly built Tropical enclosure. In fact, the Tropical Gondwanaland is over 30

LEIPZIG TRAVEL GUIDE

m in height and spans an area larger than 2 football pitches. This rainforest habitat has over 40 animal species as exhibits and nearly 500 species of plants and trees. Interactive activities in this enclosure allow visitors to climb trees, follow trails, and even float in the river.

The zoo is divided into a number of sections – Tropical Gondwanaland, Asia, Africa, South America, and Pongoland – dedicated to the great apes. There is also the Founder's Garden past the old gate where one can see the handwriting of Ernest Pinkert – the founder of the zoo. The species in the zoo include invertebrates, amphibians, fish, birds, reptiles, and mammals. Rare exhibits include the electric eel, blue poison dart frog, red piranha, bamboo shark, flamingo, ibis, macaw, Komodo dragon, anaconda, python, armadillo, and the red panda.

The zoo also has a photography stall and a souvenir shop.

The zoo is open from 9 am to 7 pm every day. There is an entry fee of €18.50. Discounts are available for children, groups, and in the winter months (Jan to March).

🌐 Museum in the Round Corner

The Museum in der Runde Ecke or the Museum in the Round Corner is named after its literal position – at the round corner on the intersection of 2 streets – Dittrichring and Goerdellerring. It is housed in the former district headquarters of the Stasi – the East German Secret Service. The museum is dedicated to highlight the adverse effects of socialist dictatorship and the dangers of a totalitarian government.

LEIPZIG TRAVEL GUIDE

The Stasi headquarters is symbolic to house this museum. Many of the original interiors have been kept intact to give the visitors an authentic feel of the terrifying atmosphere during the communist regime. With the exposed cable ducts, worn out wallpaper, and Linoleum floors, history is not only seen but also felt in this museum. It is believed that the building was used by the Gestapo before it was handed over to the Soviet army after the World War II. It was later used by the Stasi from 1950 until 1989. During these 49 years, the building became a place of terror for many citizens. In 1989, after the fall of the Berlin Wall, the citizens demanded the 'house of horror' to be converted to a museum – a demand that was met in the following year. The German government still stores a large volume of Stasi files in the building. Any German citizen can request a search to find

LEIPZIG TRAVEL GUIDE

out if the Stasi had a file on him, and can even look into the contents of the file, if there is one.

The museum has a huge collection of exhibits from the 'Stasi era'. The permanent exhibition is recreated in authentic surroundings as if more of a memorial than a museum.

Surveillance devices, forged passports, counterfeit stamps, and disguise workshop – these are just some of the exhibits in the permanent section. It also introduces the ideologies of the Stasi and their administrative structure. Also a part of the main museum is the Execution Site. The site is separated from the main building and can be accessed though the Arndt Road. Another interesting exhibit separated from the main building is the Permanent Pillar Exhibition. 20 pillars –

LEIPZIG TRAVEL GUIDE

made from metal from the GDR border fortifications – have been put up in 20 locations across the city signifying the sites where the famous Peaceful Revolution took place that brought down the dictatorship regime in 1989.

The Bunker Museum is a part of this museum and is located 30 km east of Leipzig, in Machern. It was the emergency command center of the Stasi commander. Spread over 5.2 hectares, visitors can see some of the most well preserved bunkers that were built in the late 1960s. The bunkers were hidden under a holiday complex. All the bunkers are now open to the public as a part of the museum.

The Museum is open every day from 10 am to 6 pm. There is no entry fee but donations are accepted.

LEIPZIG TRAVEL GUIDE

LEIPZIG TRAVEL GUIDE

Budget Tips

Accommodation

Gastehaus Leipzig

Wachterstrasse 32

04107 Leipzig

Tel: 49 341 1406 3131

http://www.gaostchaus-leipzig.de/en/guest-house/

Located between the New Town Hall and the Johannapark, the Gastehaus is a 3 star property which has an old world charm. The look and feel of the guesthouse perfectly blends with the historic character of its surroundings. The city center is about a 5 minute walk from the guesthouse. It is a non smoking property. There is a car park facility for guests. There is also an in-house restaurant.

LEIPZIG TRAVEL GUIDE

There are 8 rooms and 2 apartments in the complex. All rooms are ensuite and have telephone, TV, hairdryer, and writing desk. Room rates start from €65.

Mercure Leipzig am Johannisplatz

Stephanstrasse 6

04103 Leipzig

Tel: 49 341 97790

http://www.mercure.com/gb/hotel-5406-mercure-hotel-leipzig-am-johannisplatz/index.shtml

Located close to the Gewandhaus and the Leipzig Opera, the hotel is a 4 star property with 174 guestrooms. Facilities include 24 hr reception, multilingual staff, safe deposit, and luggage storage. There is high speed Wi-Fi.

The property has an onsite lounge, restaurant, and a wellness center.

The ensuite rooms have cable TV, bathtubs, writing desks, minibar, and manual temperature control. Room rates start from €59.

Hotel Adler

Portitzerstrasse 10

4318 Leipzig

Tel: 49 341 23 29 366

http://www.hoteladler-leipzig.de/en/home/index.html

The Hotel Adler is a 3 star property located east of the city center in a quiet neighborhood. It is minutes from the Grassi Museum and the Botanical Garden.

Facilities of the hotel include 24 hr reception, multilingual staff, travel desk, express check in, safe deposit, and luggage storage. There is free Wi-Fi. The hotel has a terrace, a restaurant, and designated smoking areas.

The ensuite rooms have LCD TV, complimentary toiletries, bathtubs or showers, sofa beds, and telephone. Room rates start from €45.

Hotel Admiral Leipzig

Georg-Schwarz Strasse 33-35

04177 Leipzig

Tel: 49 341 448 03 10

http://www.regency-leipzig.de/index.php?Site=switch&Lang=en

The hotel is a 3.5 star property located close to the

LEIPZIG TRAVEL GUIDE

Museum at the Round Corner and the Red Bull Arena.

This cosmopolitan hotel has a 24 hr reception, multilingual staff, express check in, and porter and room service. There is free Wi-Fi. The hotel also has a bar, restaurant, and a wellness center.

The 50 ensuite rooms have cable TV, complimentary toiletries, minibar, writing desk, hair dryer, and safe. Room rates start from €66.

Hotel Royal International

Richard Wagner Strasse 10

04109 Leipzig

Tel: 49 341 23 10 060

http://www.royal-leipzig.de/en/hotel/index.html

The hotel is a 4 star property located close to the Old

LEIPZIG TRAVEL GUIDE

Town Hall. It is housed in a beautiful Renaissance styled building with chic interior décor. The hotel has a 24 hr reception and room service. There is a multilingual staff, travel desk, free Wi-Fi, concierge service, safe deposit, and luggage storage. It also has an onsite hair salon, bar, and store.

The 64 ensuite rooms have cable TV, minibar, safe, writing desk, DVD player, radio, and a kitchenette. Room rates start from €85 and include breakfast.

🌐 Places to Eat

Barfussgasschen 9

Leipzig

Tel: 49 341 960 20 78

http://www.zillstunnel.de/home.html

LEIPZIG TRAVEL GUIDE

Located close to the Old Town Hall in the city center, the Zill's Tunnel restaurant has been serving guests since 1785. The present name is being used from 1841. It has served many celebrity guests over the years. The restaurant specializes in Saxon cuisine; it also serves beer and wine. The food is reasonably priced and served in large portions. An average meal without any alcoholic drink would cost between €10 – 15.

Tobagi

Riemannstrasse 52

Leipzig

Tel: 49 341 9625 836

http://www.tobagi.de/speisekarte/

The Tobagi is a restaurant that has been serving delicious

LEIPZIG TRAVEL GUIDE

Korean cuisine for nearly a decade. It also serves a wide variety of sushi.

Guests can choose from the set menu or buy a la carte. There is a set menu of soup, sushi, and dessert for €12.50; for €5 more one can add a salad and a meat dish. Lunch specials are available on weekdays from 12 noon to 2 pm. The Tobagi also conducts cooking courses in sushi.

Coffe Baum

Kleine Fleischergasse 4

04109 Leipzig

Tel: 49 341 9651 319

http://www.coffe-baum.de/start/index.php

The Arabishchen Coffe Baum or the Arabic Coffee House

LEIPZIG TRAVEL GUIDE

is a historic and iconic coffee house in Leipzig. Established in 1711, it is one of the oldest coffee houses in the world. Its guests have included the high and the mighty like King Augustus the Strong, Johann Sebastian Bach, Robert Schumann, Richard Wagner, and Napoleon Bonaparte! Housed in a building with a neo-Renaissance façade, the Coffee House also has a museum focusing on coffee culture in the Saxon state. The café serves a variety of Viennese, French, and Arabic coffee, along with cake, pie, and a variety of fruits.

Zest

Bornaische Strasse 54

04277 Leipzig

Tel: 49 341 231 9126

http://www.zest-leipzig.de/tvzw.html

LEIPZIG TRAVEL GUIDE

The Zest serves vegetarian and vegan cuisine. It serves soups, salads, sandwiches, burgers, and a variety of desserts. It also serves beer and wine. Dishes include lasagna in beet root puree and argan oil, orange cucumber strawberry salad, potato tortilla, gargara sub, and a variety of soy dishes. Desserts include chilled Mirabelle soup with ice-cream and bergamot sorbet. An average meal without drinks would cost about €15 – 20 per person.

Villers

Trondlinring 8

04105 Leipzig

Tel: 49 341 1400

http://www.restaurant-villers.de/en

Located in an 18th century salon with an elegant Neoclassical décor, the Villers is a restaurant for those with exquisite taste and wanting to splurge.

This fine dining restaurant serves German and International cuisine along with a strong selection of 200 wines. Set meal menus are available for 4-course (€66), 5-course (€77), and 6-course (€88). Guests can also order from the a la carte menu. An average meal without drinks would cost around €35 – 40 per person.

🌐 Shopping

Christmas Market

The Leipziger Weinachtsmarkt or Leipzig Christmas Market is the most popular seasonal market in the city. Opening in the last week of November, the market receives a huge footfall from the locals and visitors until its closing on Christmas Eve. It is less of a market and more of a festival with musical events, carnivals, Ferris wheel, children's rides, and plenty of food vendors. From food to handicrafts, the Christmas Market is a great place to buy traditional items. The market is set up near the Old Town Hall and its adjoining streets.

Flea Market

Leipzig has a number of flea markets that sell a wide variety of antiques. Spread across the Fairground at Cottaweg, it is the ideal place to hunt for bargain items, especially jewelry, tableware, antiques, and silverware. It is usually open in the summer months on weekends from 9 am to 5 pm.

Central Station Promenade

The Leipzig main railway station is one of the largest in Europe with 28 platforms. The station has a huge shopping promenade with 142 shops spread across 3 floors. It also has 2 levels of low-cost car parking as an incentive to lure in buyers. The stores in the promenade range from local retailers to some major international brands. The promenade, unlike most other malls, is open on Sundays.

Hofe am Bruhl

130 stores spread over 22300 sq m of shopping space - that is what this newly refurbished shopping center has to offer. It is located at Richard Wagner Platz. The place originally had the Bruhl trading houses which were replaced by a shopping center. The old shopping center made way for the new one in 2010. Brands present in the mall include H&M, Media Markt, and Promod. It is open Monday to Friday from 10 am to 8 pm.

Nova Eventis

Located in Gunthersdorf, this is one of the largest shopping centers of Germany. It not only has a huge number of stores, restaurants, and cafes, but also a kid's playing zone, an upside-down crazy playhouse, an ice skating rink, an indoor climbing forest, and a bumper boat pool.

It is connected by Bus 131 from Hauptbahnhof. For those planning to drive, parking is not an issue as it has free parking spaces for 2500 vehicles! It is open from 10 am to 8 pm – Monday to Saturday, with extended hours on Friday.

Know Before You Go

Entry Requirements

By virtue of the Schengen agreement, travellers from other countries in the European Union do not need a visa when visiting Germany. Visitors from Australia, Canada and the USA, do not require a visa, provided their stay does not exceed 90 days and that their passports are valid for at least three months after their stay in Germany ends. Travellers requiring a Schengen visa will be able to enter Germany with it multiple times within a 6 month period, if their stay does not exceed 90 days. They will also need to prove that they have sufficient funds to cover the duration of their stay. For a stay exceeding 90 days, non-EU visitors will need to apply for a temporary residence permit.

Health Insurance

Citizens of other EU countries are covered for emergency health care in Germany. UK residents, as well as visitors from Switzerland are covered by the European Health Insurance Card (EHIC), which can be applied for free of charge. Germany has excellent health care facilities, but emergency medical care can be expensive and will not be covered by the public health insurance of most non-European countries so health insurance cover should be obtained before leaving home. Visitors from non-Schengen countries will need to show proof of private health insurance that is valid for the duration of their stay in Germany (that offers at least €37,500 coverage), as a requirement of their visa application process.

🌐 Travelling with Pets

Germany participates in the Pet Travel Scheme (PETS) which allows UK residents to travel with their pets without requiring quarantine upon re-entry. When travelling with pets from another European Union country, your pet will need to have the correct documentation in the form of a pet passport. Certain conditions will need to be met. The animal will have to be microchipped and up to date with rabies vaccinations. Your pet will need to have had a rabies vaccination at least 21 days before your departure for Germany. If travelling from a high risk country, you will also need to submit the results of a Blood Titer test taken one month after vaccination and at least 3 months before your travel date. The animal needs to be identified either with a microchip or have an identifying tattoo.

LEIPZIG TRAVEL GUIDE

🌐 Airports

There are two airports that serve the international gateway of Berlin. **Berlin Tegel Airport** (TXL) is the larger of the two and the 4th busiest airport in Germany. Originally a military base, it was used in the Berlin Airlift operation in 1949. Towards the end of the 1950s, it began to replace Tempelhof Airport. The other main airport servicing Berlin is **Berlin Schönefeld Airport**, (SXF), once the major airport servicing East Berlin. Frankfurt Airport (FRA) is the busiest **Frankfurt Airport** (FRA) is the busiest airport in Germany and the third busiest in Europe. Located about 12km southwest of Frankfurt, it connects visitors with the densely populated Frankfurt/Rhine-Main region. Frankfurt was home to the world's first airport and airline in 1908, but this was replaced by the current airport around 1936 when it grew too small to handle demand for air traffic. There are two main terminals, as well as a first class terminal used by Lufthansa. **Munich Airport** (MUC) is the second busiest airport in Germany and provides access to the region of Bavaria. It is located about 28.5km northeast of the historical part of Munich. **Düsseldorf Airport** (DUS) is the 3rd busiest airport in Germany and provides access to the sprawling metropolis of the Rhine-Ruhr Region. It lies about 7km north of Düsseldorf and 20km from Essen. **Hamburg Airport** (HAM) is the 5th busiest airport in Germany. Located about 8.5km north of the center of Hamburg, it provides access to the north

LEIPZIG TRAVEL GUIDE

of Germany. **Stuttgart Airport** (STR) is located about 13km from the city of Stuttgart. It is an important base for Germanwings and provides connections to several European cities, as well as Atlanta in the USA and Abu Dhabi. **Cologne Bonn Airport** (CGN) provides access to Cologne, the 4th largest city in Germany and Bonn, former capital of West Germany. Founded as a military airfield in 1913, it was opened to civilian aviation in the early 1950s. **Nuremberg Airport** (NUE) is the second busiest airport in the region of Bavaria and provides connections between Germany and the Mediterranean, Egypt and the Canary Islands. **Leipzig/Halle Airport** (LEJ) connects travellers to Leipzig, Halle and other destinations in Saxony in the eastern part of Germany. Additionally it serves as an important cargo hub. Access to the southwest of Germany and particularly Freiburg, can also be gained via **EuroAirport Basel Mulhouse Freiburg**, (BSL) an international airport located on the border between France and Switzerland and near the border of Germany. It is operated by both countries with two additional German board members.

🌐 Airlines

Lufthansa is the largest airline in Europe and controls one of the largest passenger fleets in the world, consisting of around 280 aircrafts. It provides connections to almost 200 international destinations in 78 different countries across Europe, Africa,

LEIPZIG TRAVEL GUIDE

Asia and North and South America. The group was founded in 1955. Lufthansa CityLine resulted from the absorption of the regional airline, Ostfriesische Lufttaxi by Lufthansa. Air Berlin is the second largest airline in Germany and the 8th largest in Europe. Condor Flugdienst is Germany's third largest airline and is partnered with the British group Thomas Cook, as well as Lufthansa, its parent company. It flies to destinations in the Mediterranean, Asia, Africa, North and South America as well as the Caribbean. Germanwings and Eurowings are low-cost subsidiaries of Lufthansa, currently being merged and integrated into a combined enterprise. TUIfly is an airline operated by the tourism group TUI Travel. It is based at Hanover Airport with bases at several other German cities including Frankfurt, Munich, Cologne, Düsseldorf, Saarbrücken and Stuttgart. TUIfly provides connections to 39 destinations in Europe, Asia and Africa. Germania is a privately owned airline which flies to destinations within Europe, North Africa and the Middle East.

Frankfurt Airport serves as a hub for Lufthansa, Lufthansa CityLine, Condor and Aerologic. Berlin Tegel Airport serves as a hub for Air Berlin and Germanwings. Berlin Schönefeld Airport serves as a focus city for EasyJet and Condor. Düsseldorf Airport serves as a hub for Air Berlin, Eurowings and Germanwings. Munich Airport serves as a hub for Lufthansa, Lufthansa CityLine, Condor and Air Dolomiti. Stuttgart Airport also serves as a hub for Germanwings.

LEIPZIG TRAVEL GUIDE

Cologne Bonn Airport serves as an important European hub for UPS and FedEx Express. Additionally it is a hub for Eurowings and Germanwings. Leipzig/Halle Airport serves as a hub for Aerologic and DHL Aviation.

🌐 Currency

The currency of Germany is the Euro. It is issued in notes in denominations of €500, €200, €100, €50, €20, €10 and €5. Coins are issued in denominations of €2, €1, 50c, 20c, 10c, 5c, 2c and 1c.

🌐 Banking & ATMs

Using ATMs (Geldautomaten, as they are known in Germany), to withdraw money is simple if your ATM card is compatible with the MasterCard/Cirrus or Visa/Plus networks. Deutschebank is affiliated to Barclays, Bank of America, Scotiabank (of Canada), China Construction Bank, BNP Paribas (of France) and Westpac (of Australia and New Zealand), which means account holders of those bank groups should not be charged transaction fees when using the facilities of Deutschebank in Germany. Bear in mind that third party ATMs, however convenient, will also charge a higher transaction fee. Be sure to advise your bank of your travel plans and inquire about whether your bank card is compatible with German ATM machines.

🌐 Credit Cards

Most Germans prefer using cash when shopping and you may find the credit card option being being unavailable in many of the country's smaller shops, restaurants and guesthouses. Larger hotels and restaurants should accept credit card transactions. Shops will usually display a sign indicating which credit cards are accepted. The most popular credit cards are MasterCard, and its European affiliate, the Eurocard as well as Visa. Most German facilities are compliant with the new chip-and-pin debit and credit cards and may not be able to handle older magnetic strip cards.

🌐 Reclaiming VAT

If you are not from the European Union, you may be able to claim back VAT (Value Added Tax) paid on your purchases in Germany. The VAT rate in Germany is 19 percent and this can be claimed back on your purchases, if certain conditions are met. Only purchases of €25 and over qualify for a VAT refund. To qualify, you need to ask the shop assistant for export papers and this needs to be submitted to the Customs office at your port of exit, along with the receipt and a passport to prove residence outside the European Union. Customs officers will also want to inspect the goods in question to ascertain that they are unused. Once the export papers have been stamped, they can be sent to the shop where you bought the goods for a VAT refund. For a service fee, you can also get a cash refund from the offices of Global Blue, TaxfreeWorldwide or Premier Tax Free.

🌐 Tipping Policy

In German restaurants, you should tip your waiter around 10 percent or a little more if the service is excellent. This should be given to the waiter in cash, rather than left on the table when you depart. It is customary to tip porters in German hotels between €1 and €3 per bag. Tip your housekeeper between €3 and €5 per night and reward an unusually helpful concierge. Tip your tour guide 10 percent (although some tour guides may request a positive TripAdvisor review instead, as this translates to a cash bonus in certain tour companies), give your spa attendant 5 percent and round off a taxi fare to the nearest euro.

🌐 Mobile Phones

Germany uses the GSM mobile service. This means that most UK phones and some US and Canadian phones and mobile devices will work in Germany. However, phones using the

CDMA network will not be compatible. While you could check with your service provider about coverage before you leave, using your own service in roaming mode will involve additional costs. The alternative is to purchase a German SIM card to use during your stay in Germany. Until recently, Germany had four mobile networks, Deutsche Telekom (formerly known as T-Mobile), Vodafone, O2 and E-plus, but the latter two, O2 and E-plus have been acquired by Telefonica and are in the process of being merged into a single brand. A huge variety of packages for different types of usage are available from representatives and subsidiaries of each of these. Deutsche Telekom has two starter pack options - data only and voice and data - from €9.95, which includes €10 credit. For the same price, you can buy a Vodafone CallYa SIM, which also offers a basic €10 credit. You can buy your E-plus SIM card from gas (petrol) stations and retail outlets from €10, with a €5 bonus credit.

Dialling Code

The international dialling code for Germany is +49.

Emergency Numbers

Police: 110

Fire Rescue: 112

Medical Emergencies: 112

LEIPZIG TRAVEL GUIDE

Master Card: 0800 819 1040

Visa: 0800 811 8440

🌐 Public Holidays

1 January: New Year's Day

6 January: Day of the Epiphany

March/April: Good Friday

March/April: Easter Monday

1 May: Labour Day

May: Ascension Day

May: Whit Monday

May/June: Corpus Christi

3 October: Day of German Unity

31 October: Day of Reformation

1 November: All Saints Day

25 December: Christmas Day

26 December: St Stephen's Day

🌐 Time Zone

In the winter season from the end of October to the end of March, Germany's official time zone is Central European Time, which is Greenwich Mean Time/Coordinated Universal Time (GMT/UTC) +1; Eastern Standard Time (North America) -5; Pacific Standard Time (North America) -8.

LEIPZIG TRAVEL GUIDE

🌐 Daylight Savings Time

Clocks are set forward one hour on the last Sunday of March and set back one hour on the last Sunday of October for Daylight Savings Time.

🌐 School Holidays

German school holidays are not determined nationally and vary from state to state. The academic year begins early in September and ends in mid July. There is a weeklong autumn break towards the end of October, a two-week winter vacation that includes Christmas and New Year, a short spring vacation in February and a short summer half term vacation at the beginning of June. After the end of the summer term in mid July, there is a longer vacation that lasts until the next school year begins in September.

🌐 Trading Hours

German department stores are generally open from 10am to 8pm, from Mondays to Saturdays, while supermarkets are open from 8am to 8pm from Monday to Saturdays. Most German shops are closed on Sundays and also on Christmas, Easter and Public Holidays. German banks are open from 8.30am to 4pm from Mondays to Fridays. Most of the gas stations in large urban areas and near the autobahns are open 24 hours. Museums, tourist attractions, trains and buses maintain a limited schedule on Sundays.

🌐 Driving Laws

The Germans drive on the right hand side of the road as in the USA. A driver's licence from any of the European Union member countries is valid in Germany. If you are resident of a non-EU country, you may drive on that country's license for the first six months of your stay in Germany. You may need to obtain a German translation of your driving license. The minimum driving age in Germany is 18, but most car rental companies will require renters to be at least 21. Bear in mind that the majority of cars will be stick (manual) shift and that an automatic car may be more expensive to hire. You will need to have a Green Insurance certificate as well as standard on board emergency gear like emergency triangles, a jack, spare wheel and first aid kit. German autobahns or freeways are famous for imposing no speed limit, though you may find that variable speed limits are imposed on certain sections of the road, or a 130km limit may apply where safety and congestion is a factor. At the approach of a major junction or intersection, the limit drops to 80km per hour. In urban and residential areas, the speed limit will be between 30 and 50km per hour. You will need a special sticker or Umweltplakette (which costs €6) to be able to drive in designated Green Zones. A violation of this policy may incur a fine of €40.

🌐 Smoking Laws

Germany has banned smoking from all indoor public places including restaurants and bars, although it is usually allowed in outdoor sections, such as beer gardens. While some businesses have obtained exemption in states such as Saxony, Rhineland-Pfalz and Saarland, the regulations are particularly strict in Bavaria. Fines vary according to region, but can be anything from €10 to €5000. To buy cigarettes from a vending machine, you will be required to submit some form of identification.

🌐 Drinking Laws

The legal drinking age in Germany is 16, although minors can consume beer or wine from the age of 14, if in the company of a parent or guardian. They can, however, only consume and buy distilled beverages, such as whiskey and brandy, from the age of 18. In general, Germany enjoys some of the most lenient laws towards alcohol consumption and public drinking is mostly tolerated. Some places forbid the consumption of alcohol on trains and transit. Alcohol can be bought from a variety of places including restaurants, bars, grocery stores, garages and even newspaper vendors. Additionally the price of alcohol is the lowest in Europe.

 Electricity

Electricity: 230 volts

Frequency: 50 Hz

German electricity sockets use the Type C and F plugs, which feature two round pins or prongs. If travelling from the USA, you will need a power converter or transformer to convert the voltage from 230 to 110, to avoid damage to your appliances. The latest models of many laptops, camcorders, mobile phones and digital cameras are dual-voltage with a built in converter.

Tourist Information (TI)

There are Tourist and Visitor Information offices in several of the larger German cities, where you can pick up maps and local travel guides to help plan your visit. The Berlin office is at 11 Am Karlsbad; in Frankfurt, go to 56 Kaiserstrasse; in Hamburg, 7 Steinstrasse; in Munich, 1 Sendlinger Strasse; in Leipzig, 1 Richard Wagner Strasse; in Stuttgart, 1 Königstrasse; in Hannover, 8 Ernst-August-Platz; in Dusseldorf, 65b Immermannstrasse; in Bonn, 131 Adenauerallee; in Cologne, 19 Unter Fettenhennen; in Nuremberg, 3 Frauentorgraben; in Dresden, 11 Ostra-Allee and in Dortmund, 18a Königswall.

LEIPZIG TRAVEL GUIDE

🌍 Food & Drink

There are well over 1500 different types of sausage (wurst) made in Germany. These are divided into four basic types - raw wurst, cooked wurst, scalded wurst and, of course, the famous bratwurst, which can be found in over 50 regional varieties. Wienerwurst is a relative of the American frankfurter, but do not confuse the American frankfurter with the German one, a smoked sausage of pure pork which is regional speciality of the city of Frankfurt. There is also a good selection of raw and cooked ham, known locally as schinken. With 400 different types of cheese, dairy lovers will also be spoilt for choice, especially in the pre-alpine region of Allgäu in Bavaria, which produces the majority of the country's cheeses. A traditional German stew is eintopf, so named as it is prepared in a single pot. Enjoy Berlin cuisine with a delicious helping of eisbein, pickled ham hock served with sauerkraut or mashed potatoes. On the sweet side, apfelstrudel is a popular German pastry made with apples, cinnamon and raisins. If you are in Germany around Christmas time, spoil yourself with a helping of seasonal lebkuchen.

German drinking culture is synonymous with beer. The country has around 1200 breweries and more than 5000 different beer brands. In most parts of Germany, pale lager pilsner is the preferred beer, although wheat (weiss) beer is popular in Bavaria. Try a dark beer known as Altbier from Düsseldorf. As an after dinner digestive, Germans enjoy Schnapps, a clear, strong fruit-flavored alcoholic drink or herbal liqueurs such as Jägermeister and Underberg. Germany has some decent wine varietals from grapes that are grown along the banks of the Rheine and the Mosel. For a novelty, try an Eiswein (ice wine), a sweet dessert wine produced from grapes that were frozen while still on the vine. Apfelwein or cider is a popular alternative to beer and can be combined with sparkling water for Sauer Gespritzer or lemonade for Sussgespritzer. A local variety from Frankfurt called Speierling adds berries to the usual apfelwein. On the non-alcoholic side, Germans are also fond of fruit juice and mix this with sparkling water, especially apple juice. This particular mix is known as apfelschorle. Additionally, Germans love strong, flavorful coffee, which is hardly surprising since the coffee filter was invented in Germany.

 Websites

http://www.germany.travel/en/index.html

http://www.german-way.com/

http://www.howtogermany.com/

http://www.germany-tourism.net/

LEIPZIG TRAVEL GUIDE

https://www.deutschland.de/en/topic/life/mobility-travel/tourism

http://germanyiswunderbar.com/

http://wikitravel.org/en/Germany

Printed in Great Britain
by Amazon